KIDS' MAGIC SECRETS

SHH! Don't tell. PUH-LEEZE

KIDS' MAGIC
SECRETS

SIMPLE MAGIC TRICKS
& WHY THEY WORK

Text by
LORIS BREE

Illustrations by
MARLIN BREE

MARLOR PRESS, INC.
Saint Paul, MN

KIDS' MAGIC SECRETS

By Loris Bree
Illustrations by Marlin Bree

ISBN 978-1-892147-08-0
Copyright 2003 by Loris and Marlin Bree

Printed in U.S.A.

MARLOR PRESS, INC.
4304 Brigadoon Drive
Saint Paul, MN 55126

CONTENTS

BODY OF MAGIC

ALL WET

SCARF IT UP

AMAZINGLY MYSTERIOUS

* is the easiest task and
*** is the most difficult

Magic isn't just MAGIC.

IT'S tons of FUN!

INTRODUCTION

Practice. Much depends on your being able to do a trick smoothly, quickly, and without hesitating. When you hesitate or stop, your audience will get a clue to detect how you're doing the trick.

Never repeat a trick. When you do it a second time, your audience starts looking for clues and are more likely to see how it's done. Sometimes you might want to do another similar trick. If someone asks you to repeat a card trick, for example, don't do the same trick but do another one.

Even simple tricks require skill. Doing these tricks requires talents that are important to learning to do other things. If you really want to learn a magic trick and learn to do it well, you'll be able to use these skills for other activities, in school, playing games, and getting along with your family.

They require physical dexterity and good memory. The ability to communicate is extremely important.

A magician is an entertainer. Often the only thing that keeps the attention of the audience is the ability of the magician to talk to them.

Magic tricks usually have an underlying concept that explains why they work. You really don't need a magic wand to make things happen. Magic wands or other items are used to keep the attention of the audience focused where you want it to be.

The actual trick often works because of a scientific or mathematical model.

BANANA SUR-PRISE

ZOW! YOU PEEL BACK A BANANA -- AND IT'S ALREADY SLICED

Your audience will see you peel an ordinary banana. When you pull back the peeling, the banana will already be sliced into chunks. *Incredible*.

YOU WILL NEED

1. A ripe **banana**

2. A **plate or bowl**

3. A **clean needle and thread**

SEW RIDGE TO RIDGE

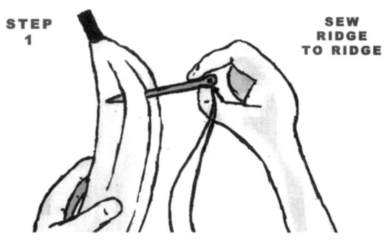

1. **On the day of your magical appearance but before your audience arrives** you can prepare your banana. Stick the threaded needle into a spot on a ridge of the banana, near the top (Step 1). Bring the needle out at the next ridge but leave a three to five inch tail of thread hanging out from the first hole.

TOP VIEW

STEP 1

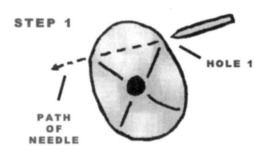

HOLE 1

PATH OF NEEDLE

2. Push the needle back into the second hole (Step 2) and bring it back out at the next ridge. Put the needle back into the third hole and bring it out at the next ridge. Continue to follow these steps until you bring the needle out at the first hole.

STEP 2

HOLE 1

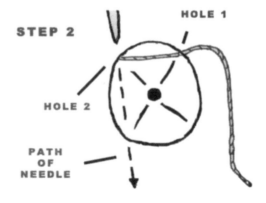

HOLE 2

PATH OF NEEDLE

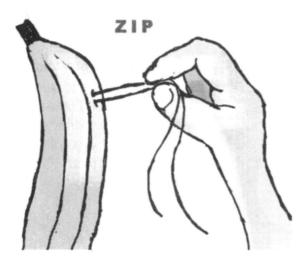

ZIP

3. Hold both ends of the thread in your hand and pull the thread until it comes out of the hole. You've just made a secret slice in the banana. Nobody can see the tiny needle hole

4. Now make another invisible slice about an inch below the first hole. Repeat the steps. You can slice the entire banana or only make four or five slices.

5. Put the needle and thread out of sight. Leave the banana and plate on the table or in a box with your other magic supplies.

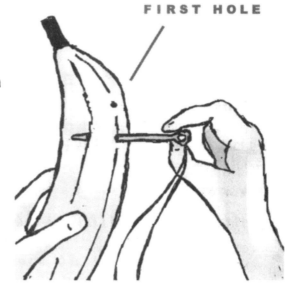

FIRST HOLE

6. When it is time for your trick, **tell your audience:** *"I really like my bananas sliced but my mother doesn't want me fooling around with knives. I think I've finally solved my problem. I use magic."*

7. Hold up the banana and **say,** *"BANANA, BE SLICED."* Then you wave your hand back and forth and up and down around the banana. If you want to, you can **repeat,** *"BANANA, BE SLICED."*

8. Holding the banana over a plate or napkin, begin to peel the banana. As you peel the slices will fall on the plate. Wow. *Look at their faces!*

9. **Extra fun step:** If you are very careful to only use a fine needle and fine thread, you can let someone from the audience look at the banana *before you begin* so they can see that it is not peeled or sliced.

HOW THE TRICK WORKS

TASTY TOO!

This uses a mathematical or scientific concept called **sectioning.** It means to divide something into slices or parts. By putting a thread in at a banana seam, you divide the fruit, section by section. Tension on the thread cuts the section inside without peeling the banana. The result? To the audience, it's *magic!*

COINS IN A BOTTLE

You show your audience some coins and a bottle. You put a card across the bottle, put the coins on top. You challenge them to get the coins into the bottle without touching them. They can't do it. Then you show them how. *Stupendous!*

YOU MAKE COINS FLIP INTO A BOTTLE *WITHOUT* TOUCHING THEM

YOU WILL NEED

1. An **empty bottle or jar.** The bottle opening must be larger than the coins.

2. A **square piece of cardboard,** like a file card or a square cut from a cereal or tissue box. Cut your card so that it is square (3 x 3 inches is great) and larger than the bottle opening.

3. Two or three **coins**

HOW THE TRICK WORKS

1. You show the audience a bottle and some coins. You might even ask for coins from your audience. Tell them that you'd like two or three pennies or nickels.

2. When you have your coins and the bottle, hold them up for the audience to see. Tell them you will put the bottle on the table and will place the coins so they will leap into the bottle without being touched by you.

3. Put the bottle on the table, hold up the card and wave it at the audience as you place it on top of the bottle. Then place the coins on the cardboard just above the bottle opening. Tell the audience that you will move the cardboard from the top of the jar and get the coins inside without touching the coins or the jar.

COINS

CARDBOARD

FLICK!

4. Flick or snap the edge of the card, quickly and sharply, with your finger. The card should snap out from between the coins and the bottle. The coins drop into the bottle *without your touching them.*

GASP!
HOW'D
SHE DO
THAT?

5. You need to practice this several times until the coins always drop in. If the card moves a little too slowly the coins will fly after the card instead of dropping into the bottle.

FLICK!

FLICK!

HOW THE TRICK WORKS:

EASY
WHEN
YOU KNOW
HOW!

The coins are sitting on top of the card. Inertia wants the coins to stay still. The card snaps away *so quickly* that the coins are not able to follow the card. **Gravity** pulls them down into the bottle.

GHOSTLY GLASSES

NAMES APPEAR ON GLASSES, AS IF BY MAGIC

You **say a magic word** and name one of your guests as you pick up an ordinary glass. Put the glass in the refrigerator. At the end of your magic show, you remove each glass, and as each guest's name appears on the frosty side, you give the glass to them. *Surprising!*

YOU'LL NEED

1. A **glass** for each of your guests.
2. A small **jar** or container
3. **Liquid detergent**
4. A **tray**
5. A **drink** for your guests. This can be kool-aid, lemonade or a soda

HOW IT WORKS

WRITE
WRITE

1. **Before your guests arrive,** put just a little bit of water in the small glass or container. Add a drop of liquid detergent. With your finger, carefully print the first name of one of your guests on a glass. Continue until you have printed the name of each of your guests on one of the glasses.

HINT: If you use glasses that look different, you'll need to remember which name you printed on which glass. If the glasses are identical, it won't matter. Put the glasses on your table and allow them to dry so the printing won't show.

FREE
DRINKS?

2. **When your guests arrive** and are seated to watch your magic, tell them that you are preparing drinks for after the show and you want to be sure that everyone has a glass. Then tell them that the glasses are magic glasses

3. Pick up each glass and **say**, *"Alakazam, this glass is (Bill's) glass."* If you have a magic wand or want to use a special magic wave, you can then wave over the glass before you put it on the tray. Continue as you pick up each glass, fill the tray and name each guest. If you have different glasses you'll want to be sure you remember which glass is for each guest. Some of the guests may remember which glass was supposed to be theirs.

4. Tell the guests that you will now put the glasses in the refrigerator to cool so the drinks will be very cool and delicious. Then you or your helper will take the tray to the refrigerator or freezer. The glasses should be in the refrigerator for at least 30 minutes.

5. **At the end of the show** bring the glasses directly from the refrigerator to the table. The glasses should get frosty and the names should appear as clear lines in the frost on the side of the glass. *Ghostly magic!* **Don't fill the glasses** until each person has found his or her name in the frost.

You need to practice this trick several times before you do it before guests in order to be sure that you're mixing your writing solution correctly (not very much water) and to see that the glasses get cold enough to get frosty. **EXTRA TRICK:** If you live where you have cold winters, you may do a variation of this by writing a message on a cold window and blowing on the window when you want your message to appear. Once again, you have to try this and practice to be sure it works on your windows.

WHY THIS WORKS

When **water vapor** in the air condenses and freezes on a cold surface like a glass that has been in the freezer, it creates frost or ice crystals. The detergent creates a slippery surface that makes it more difficult for ice crystals to form. That's why names appear (everything but the slippery surface gets frosted.)

PAPER CLIP FLIP

PAPER CLIPS MAGICALLY LINK UP IN MIDAIR!

You **fold a dollar bill** and put two paper clips on it, then you pull the bill through the paper clips until the clips fly off the bill and land on your table linked together. *Incredible!*

YOU'LL NEED

1. A **Dollar bill**

2. **Two paper clips** (jumbo size are best but regular size will do)

HOW IT WORKS

1. **Hold the bill up, between your hands**, so your audience can easily see it. Tell them that you are going to show them how to connect two paper clips using a dollar bill.

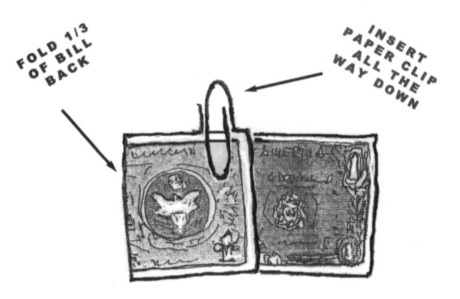

2. Fold 1/3 of the back of the bill over the front. Use a paper clip to hold it there, with the **clip over the number one** on the bill. Push the clip all the way down against the top of the bill. Tell your audience what you are doing but in a simpler way. **Say**, *"I'm going to fold the bill and put a paper clip here."* Don't tell them exactly where, though. Remember you hope they won't be able to do it by themselves when they go home.

FOLD BILL TO RIGHT

FOLD   **SIDE VIEW**

3. **Now turn the bill around** so you are looking at the other side but the clip should still be at the top of the bill. Fold the left end of the bill to the right and insert the second paper clip from the top at the end of the bill over the number one. This time, just clip the two front folds, not the back of the bill. Look at the illustrations to see how it should look. As you do this you **say,** *"Now I'll fold the bill again and put the second clip here."* See the side view (left) and top view (below).

Top view shows how clips fit over folded dollar bill. Note that the second clip fits over the front and second folds, but not the back of the bill. The first paper clip fits on the back of the bill and on the second fold.

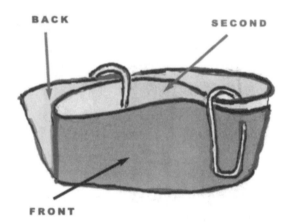

BACK   SECOND

FRONT

TOP VIEW

4. Now carefully hold both ends of the bill and pull them so the clips slide closer together and the bill begins to unfold. Say, *"Now I'm going to unfold the bill."* Try a joke like, *"I hope this works. I can't afford to lose any more bills."*

5. When the bills reach the point where they are almost together, **give** the ends a sharp tug with your hands. The bill will open out and the paper clips will fly across the table. When you show your audience, they'll be linked together.

6. Practice this so you can do it smoothly and quickly for your audience. When you present your magic performance to your audience, only do it once. Don't let them talk you into doing it again. For another trick, try the Paper Clip and Rubber Band Connection

WHY THIS WORKS

The folds in the paper allow the clips to slide into each other and connect. Your speed and the fact that this is not a common sight create an illusion of difficulty. *Fun, huh?*

HE DID IT AGAIN

FWIP!

TWO
PAPER CLIPS
HANG FROM
RUBBER BAND

PAPER CLIPS & RUBBER BAND

YOU LINK PAPER CLIPS INTO A RUBBER BAND ON THE FLY. *INGENIOUS!*

You **fold a dollar bill** and put two paper clips and a rubber band on it, then you pull the bill through the paper clips. This time the clips do not fly off. Instead the rubber band is looped around your bill and clips are hanging from the rubber band. *Incredible!*

YOU'LL NEED

1. A **dollar bill**
2. Two **paper clips** (jumbo size are best but regular size will do)
3. A **rubber band** slightly longer than the bill's width so part of the band hangs below the bill

HOW IT WORKS

Begin by following steps 1 and 2 of the *Paper Clip Flip*.

1. Before you turn the bill around, slip the rubber band over the unfolded right side of the bill. Say, *"This time I'll add a rubber band."*

RUBBER BAND

SIDE VIEW

2. Now turn the bill around so you are looking at the other side. Follow Step 3 of the Paper Clip Flip. Then you say, *"Now I'll fold the bill again and put the second clip here."* Your bill should look like this. (*See side view*)

RUBBER BAND

TOP VIEW: Note that the rubber band lies between the front and second folds of the dollar bill.

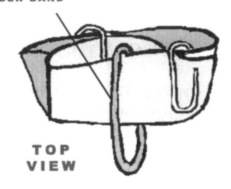

TOP VIEW

PULL, PULL

FWIP!

3. Now carefully hold both ends of the bill and pull them so the clips slide closer together and the bill begins to unfold. **Say**, *"Now I'm going to unfold the bill."* This time your joke might be *"I hope this doesn't injure anyone. Maybe you should take cover if you're in the front row."*

4. When the bills reach the point where they are almost together, firmly pull both ends of the bill. The bill will open out and the rubber band will stay on the bill but the paper clips will be connected in a chain at the bottom of the band. Hold the bill with the rubber band and clips up so your audience can see and be properly amazed. *You're a genius.*

5. Practice this slowly so you can see how it works. Then practice doing it smoothly and quickly for your audience. Don't do it a second time for the same audience.

WHY THIS WORKS

NEAT!

Once again you are creating an **illusion** that will seem magical to your audience but is perfectly **logical** when you see how the rubber band and clips slide together.

HOLA!

THE
HOPPING
RUBBER
BAND

ZAP! MAKE AN ORDINARY RUBBER BAND JUMP BACK AND FORTH BETWEEN YOUR FINGERS

The magician **has a rubber band around two fingers**. Then the band jumps to two different fingers and back again. Even when another band binds the tops of the fingers together, the band jumps back and forth right through the top band. *Astonishing!*

YOU'LL NEED

1. A **rubber band** that will comfortably stretch around your fingers. Try assorted bands to be sure that they're not too tight or too loose.

HOW IT WORKS

LEFT
HAND
FACES
AWAY

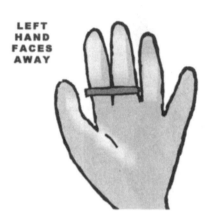

1. **On your left hand**, put a rubber band over your forefinger and your middle finger. Hold the palm side of your hand toward you. **Say:** "*I will now make this rubber band magically move through my fingers without hurting myself or the band.*

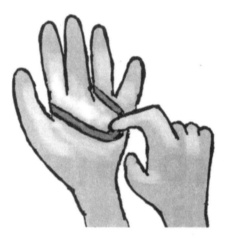

2. Pull the rubber band to show that it is solid. **Say:** "*See that this is a solid rubber band. Would you like to look at it yourself ?*" Let someone inspect it. Then put it back.

BEND FINGERS
DOWN

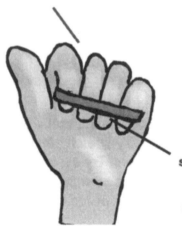

STRETCH
BAND
OVER
FOUR
FINGERS

3. When you pull it toward you a final time, bend your fingers down and **with your right hand,** stretch the band over the tips of all four fingers of your left hand.

FINGERS CLOSED

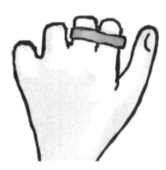

**BAND *FLIPS*
OVER FINGERS**

FWIP!

4 From the front, **your audience will see** the rubber band around only two fingers. Stop just a moment. **Say:** *"Magic band, hop, hop magic band."* Straighten your fingers. The band will absolutely jump to your ring finger and your little finger. *Wow!*

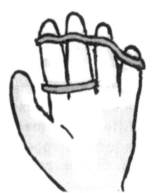

5. Take another rubber band and wrap it around the tops of the fingers so that they look tied together, like the illustration. Then do the same steps again. It'll look like the first rubber band jumps right through the top band.

6. ADDITIONAL TRICKS: You can do the same thing again and get the band to jump back to the original fingers.

WHY IT WORKS

FUN!

The jumping band is an **illusion**. It always stays around the base of the fingers, moves easily to the second fingers and never penetrates the top band.
Do it slowly and you'll see.

HOP!
HOP!

TWIN HOPPING RUBBER BANDS

WHAT COULD BE MORE FUN THAN TWO *DIFFERENT* BANDS CHANGING PLACES?

Astound your audience. This time, **you make two different rubber bands** jump to opposite fingers. *Flabbergasting!*

YOU'LL NEED

1. **Two different colored rubber bands.** Bright, contrasting colors work especially well.

HOW IT WORKS

1. Let's say you choose a red band and a blue band. (It's easier to explain if we use colors.) Place the red band around your left index and middle finger. Place the blue one around your left ring and little finger.

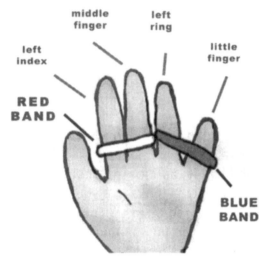

middle finger

left ring

left index

little finger

RED BAND

BLUE BAND

2. **With your left thumb**, pull out the blue band (the one that's around your left ring finger and your little finger).

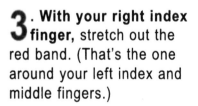

3. **With your right index finger,** stretch out the red band. (That's the one around your left index and middle fingers.)

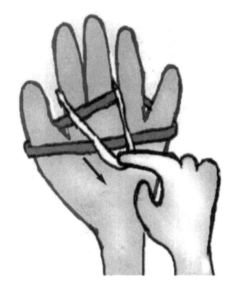

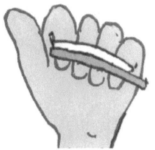

4. Close the fingers of your left hand. To the audience, it will look like a fist. In the back side of your hand, slip your fingers in the rubber bands as shown. Note that they all fit around your four fingers equally.

5. Call your audience's attention to the location of the bands, as they see them (your fist). It looks like you have the red band around only the first two fingers and the blue band only around the last two. But they'll be *surprised.*

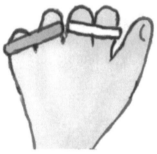

FWIP
FWIP

6. Now straighten your fingers. Zap! The bands will appear to jump to the opposite fingers.

WHY THIS WORKS

You have cleverly created an **illusion** that you can make bands jump from finger to finger. Do the trick slowly and discover how it actually works.

RING THE PENCIL

CORDS MAGICALLY GO THROUGH RINGS AND A PENCIL *WITHOUT* DAMAGE. *WOW!*

You **tie two rings to a pencil** using two shoelaces and a firm knot. Say a magic word and the strings appear to come right through the rings, leaving them on the pencil. *Unbelievable!*

YOU'LL NEED

1. **Two shoestrings** (it's easier when the laces are different colors).
2. A **pencil**
3. **Two rings** that are loaned by members of the audience
4. An audience **volunteer**

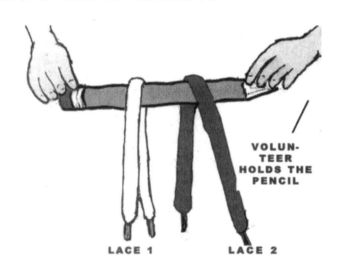

**VOLUN-
TEER
HOLDS THE
PENCIL**

LACE 1   LACE 2

1. Pick up a pencil and two shoestrings from your table. Ask for a volunteer from the audience to help with this trick.

2. Give your volunteer the pencil and ask her/him to hold it at each end. Drape the two shoelaces over the pencil. We'll call the shoelaces **Lace 1** and **Lace 2.**

LACE 1

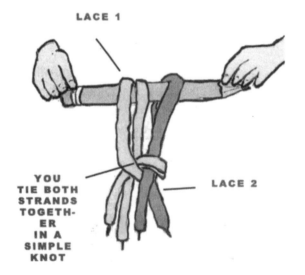

**YOU
TIE BOTH
STRANDS
TOGETH-
ER
IN A
SIMPLE
KNOT**

LACE 2

3. Then take both strands of each shoelace and tie them in a single overhand knot like the illustration. **Be sure you have Lace 1 in one hand and Lace 2 in the other.**

3. Pull the knot tight and ask the volunteer to let go of the pencil. You are now holding the laces.

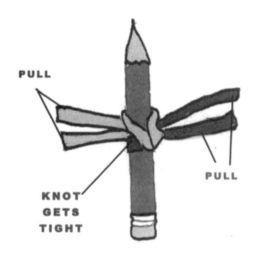

4. Hold the laces so the pencil is held by the laces in an up and down position. Pull the shoestrings tight so the pencil won't slide out. Then give the ends of the laces to the volunteer to hold.

5. Now **tell** the audience that you'll need two rings. Ask if someone will let you borrow one or two rings. Your audience will not be large so it might be a good idea if you have a friend in the audience who will be able to give you the rings if no one else provides them. Tell your friend to wait until you are sure that no one else is going to loan you a ring. (Your audience is always more enthusiastic if they are helping you with the trick.)

6. Take the rings and thread them onto the lace. Put one ring on Lace 1 on one side of the pencil and one ring on Lace 2 on the other side, as shown in the illustration.

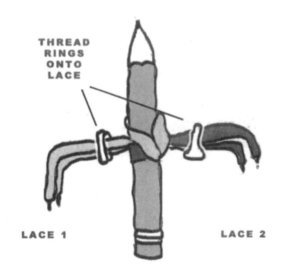

7. Now tie the rings in place. While your volunteer holds the strings, take one strand of Lace 1 and one strand of Lace 2. Tie a single knot. It doesn't matter which string of Lace 1 or Lace 2 you choose, but be sure you have one shoelace from each.

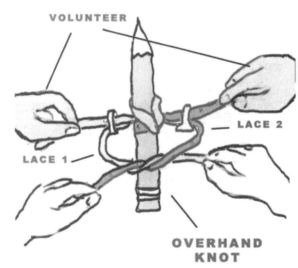

VOLUNTEER

LACE 2

LACE 1

OVERHAND KNOT

8. Pull the new knot tight, so that the rings are stuck tightly against the pencil. Give the ends of the knot back to the volunteer so that he/she is holding the ends of both shoelaces with the pencil and rings in the middle.

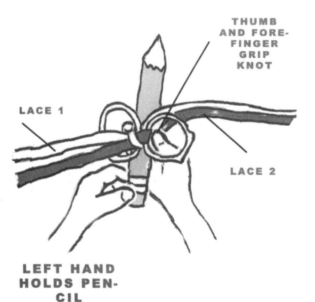

THUMB AND FORE-FINGER GRIP KNOT

LACE 1

LACE 2

LEFT HAND HOLDS PEN-CIL

9. **With your right hand** grip the knot on the pencil, hold the pencil in your left hand. Now **with your left hand** pull the pencil out of the knot.

HOLD KNOT

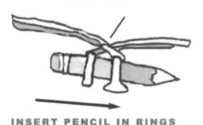

INSERT PENCIL IN RINGS

10. Continue to hold the knot with your right hand while you insert the pencil through the rings. Hold tight on the knot so it does not slip.

11. Ask your volunteer to pull on the ends of the laces and you **say** the magic word, "RINGCADABRA." Let go of the knot in your right hand. Continue to hold the pencil in your left hand. The rings will seem to go right through the laces.

RINGCADABRA

12. Hold the pencil and the rings up where your audience can see. Let your volunteer and the audience look at the pencil, rings and laces to see that there was no trick pencil or laces involved. *Ho, Ho!*

● ● ● ● ● ● ● ● ● ●

● 　　**WHY THIS WORKS**

You are using **illusion** to make it appear that the rings are firmly anchored by the knot. Actually, you have created a knot that will untie when someone pulls on each end of the laces. This leaves the rings on the pencil and the shoelaces unattached. *Fun, huh?*

● ● ● ● ● ● ● ● ● ● ● ● ● ● ● ●

THE
MAGIC
PEN

A PEN STAYS IN YOUR HANDS WITH NO *APPARENT* WAY OF STAYING UP

You fold your hands **together** and show the audience that they are empty. Then you reach down and pick up a pen from the table with your thumbs. Slowly you release your thumbs and the pen appears to stay stuck to your hands. *Inconceivable!*

YOU'LL NEED

1. A **pen** or **pencil**
2. **Two hands** *(your own)*

1. Fold your hands, intertwining your fingers. You'll want to secretly leave the middle finger of one hand loose inside your hand. If you do this carefully no one will be able to see that one finger is missing.

FINGER MISSING?
(BUT WHO WILL KNOW)

SECRET FINGER

2. Slowly pick up the pen with the thumbs of your two hands. Wrap the loose finger around the pen but continue to hold it with the thumbs. Then slowly and carefully let go of the pen with your thumbs. Appear to be very serious as you do this. *Concentrate!*

3. Zow! The pen magically seems to stay in your hands. **Explain:** "*This only works if you have magic hands.*" Be sure that the audience can't see the back of your hands. At the end, you can dramatically drop the pen or pencil, as if you have broken the magic spell.

WHY THIS WORKS

You use an **illusion** that makes it appear all of your fingers are laced together. If the trick is done well the audience won't be able to tell unless someone counts your fingers (basic math).

OH, BOY,
CARD TRICKS

MAGIC
CARD
TRICKS

TERMS & ACTIVITIES

Card deck: Usually a deck of 52 cards, in four classifications (hearts, diamonds, spades and clubs). Each card is slightly different and distinct. If you don't have a regular deck of cards but have similar cards for a game you play, you can substitute your cards for most of these tricks. Each card should be different.

Back of the card: The back of the cards should all look exactly alike so if you hold one up in your hand, the person looking at you can't tell how that card is different from the others.

Face of the card: The part that makes the card distinctive from all of the other cards in the deck. The Queen of Hearts is different from the Queen of Diamonds or the King of Hearts.

Shuffle the cards: Mixing the cards in some way so they are not in order.

Cut the cards: Picking up part of the deck that was on top and putting it on the bottom.

Fan the cards: Hold them in your hand so you are holding the bottoms together but the tops fan out (like a paper fan) and you can tell what each card is.

Key card: The one chosen: the card you are looking for; the card your volunteer thinks you couldn't possibly guess. *Ho! Ho!*

WOW. THE SECRET CARD

WHAT CARD?

YOU FIND A SECRET CARD WITHOUT EVER HAVING SEEN IT

You pick up a deck of cards, shuffle them and ask a volunteer to choose a card without showing it to you. You cut the cards, put a portion on the table, ask your friend to put her card on top of the cards on the table and then top it with rest of the cards. You invite her to cut the cards. You turn over the cards and **say**, *"the next card will be the card you picked."* You pick one card from the deck and **say** *"It was the ___."* You'll be right, of course. *Extraordinary.*

YOU'LL NEED

1. A **deck of cards**

GLANCE AT BOTTOM CARD

BOTTOM CARD IS
QUEEN OF HEARTS

HOW IT WORKS

1. When you have finished shuffling the cards, sneak a quick look at the bottom card. You have to practice so you do this quickly without your audience catching on. Remember your bottom card.

2. Ask your friend to choose a card from the entire deck. Fan out the cards for this or just let her choose from the entire deck. The card she chose is the key card. She holds this until you cut the cards.

MY CARD!

KEY CARD IS
ACE OF DIAMONDS

3. Cut the cards. Put only the top half of the deck on the table. These should be face down.

TOP HALF
OF DECK ONLY
FACE DOWN

FRIEND PLACES KEY CARD ATOP DECK ON

CARDS ON TABLE

4. Ask your friend to put her card on top of the cards on the table. The key card is now atop the deck on the table.

5. Then you put your cards on top. You have just put the card that was originally on the bottom on top of the card she chose.

6. Invite her to cut (not shuffle) the cards several times. Place the entire deck in your hand, face down.

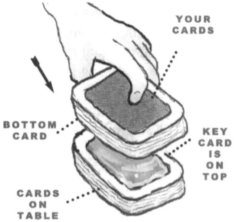

YOUR CARDS

BOTTOM CARD

KEY CARD IS ON TOP

CARDS ON TABLE

BOTTOM CARD

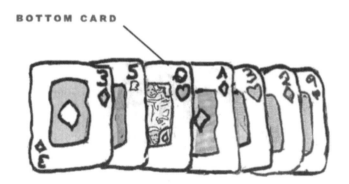

7. Turn over the cards from the deck, one at a time. Fan them out on the table so you can see them. If you turn over too many, pile up some of them but continue to show the most recent cards turned over. Watch for your bottom card but continue past it as you turn cards over, face up, on the table.

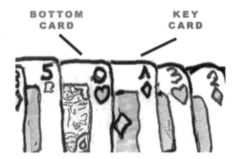

8.The key card is the card you turned over immediately after the bottom card. Remember to just keep going. Don't let your audience guess that you know you've found the bottom card or the key card.

9.After you've turned over a few more cards, **say** *"The next card I pick will be the card you chose!"* You might even bet a candy bar with your friend. Your friend will think you missed her card because it's right there, face up, in the cards already turned over, so she is sure to bet with you. *Ho, Ho!*

10. Now, stop. Go back to the cards already turned over, pick the card right after your bottom card and **say,** *"It was the (name of card!)"* and point to it. You'll be right. That's because the key card follows the bottom card.

WHY THIS WORKS

When you cut the deck you really only separate two cards. The rest of the cards stay in the same order. The **mathematical** odds are extremely high that the bottom card and the key card will stay next to each other. Since you knew which card was the bottom card, the next card up had to be the key card!

WHICH CARD?

A VOLUNTEER CHOOSES A SECRET CARD AND HIDES IT IN THE CARD DECK. YOU SAY A MAGIC WORD AND FIND IT

You **deal 21 cards,** pick a volunteer from your audience to choose a "key" card. The volunteer won't tell you which card she/he picked. Then you pick up the cards, lay them out again, and once again. After the third time, you put the cards in a pile one by one. Suddenly you stop, **say "ABRACADABRA",** turn the next card face up and it will be the card your volunteer chose. It's *prestidigitation!*

YOU'LL NEED

1. A deck of cards
2. A volunteer

BEGIN THREE COLUMNS

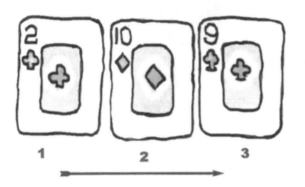

1   2   3

HOW IT WORKS

1. Deal 21 cards from your deck. You will want to make seven rows and three columns. You begin by putting three cards face up, like this.

2. Then you put another card on each of the three columns, stacking them so you can see each of the cards behind the ones you are dealing.

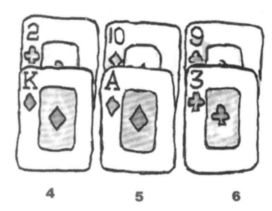

4   5   6

3. Continue until there are seven cards in each column but be sure you always deal across in three rows. (Don't try to do a column of seven at a time because your magic won't work that way.)

4. Ask a volunteer to pick a card without telling you which card she/he picked. Remind your volunteer to be careful to remember which card it is. Then ask your volunteer to tell you which column contains the secret (or key) card.

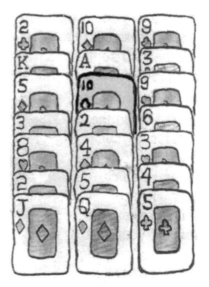

PICKS *SECOND* COLUMN

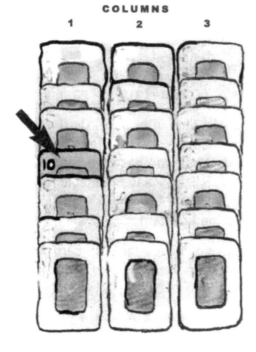

COLUMNS
1   2   3

KEY CARD MOVES TO
FIRST COLUMN

5. Then pick up the columns and make the column with the key card the second column you pick up. Don't shuffle your cards or cut them but you can show them to the audience or your volunteer. (One way to do this is to fan them out.) Then lay them out again in seven rows and three columns. Note that in this example, the key card moves to the first column. Always speak loudly so the audience can hear you.

6. Again ask the volunteer to tell you which column contains the secret card. Again pick up the cards and keep the column with the key card or secret card in the middle.

7. Deal the cards in seven rows and three columns. Again ask your volunteer to tell you which column contains the key card. Pick them up so the column with the key card is the second column you pick up. You should have done this three times.

8. Now hold the cards in your hand face down, just as you did when you dealt them in rows. This time, tell your volunteer you're going to find his/her key card using a magic word.

ABRA-
CA-
DAB-
RAI

WOW! SHE DID IT!

KEY CARD

9. Deal the cards face down, one at a time into a pile. Count the cards, to yourself, as you lay them down. Don't let your audience hear you counting out loud. When you have ten cards in the pile, tell your audience that you will now say the magic word and find the secret card. **Say** "ABRA-CA-DAB-RA" then deal the next card face up. It will be the key card.

10. Remember that your the key card will be the 11th card so count to 10 and then say the magic word and turn over the next card in your hand. *Magical.*

WHY THIS WORKS

It may seem like magic to your audience, but you are really doing a **mathematical** problem. When you have resorted the cards three times, the key card will always be the fourth card in the middle row or 11th from the beginning of the 1st or 3rd column.

FERRY ACROSS PUZZLE

YOU AMAZE YOUR AUDIENCE WITH YOUR ABILITY TO SOLVE A PROBLEM

For a change of pace, you **tell your audience a story** and ask them how to solve it. Your audience is puzzled, for it seems unsolvable. Then you demonstrate, using your cards. *Amazing cogitation!*

YOU'LL NEED

1. Playing cards (or you could draw pictures of a man, a lion, a monkey and a banana on 3-by-5 file cards).

> **Use cards to illustrate a story. Use your own picture cards or playing cards. A king could represent the man, an ace stand for the lion, a six for the monkey and a four for the bananas. Put each of them on the left side of the table. Move the cards to the right to show you are crossing the river. This is how the story goes:**

A circus performer was on his way to join the circus with his pet lion, his monkey and a sack of bananas. He came to a river where he found a small boat, just large enough to hold him and one other animal or thing. He was afraid to leave the monkey with the bananas because he would try to eat them all and get sick. He didn't want to leave the lion with the monkey because the lion might eat the monkey. *How did he get them across?"*

1.The man takes the monkey across to the other side, leaving the lion with the bananas (take the king and the six and move them to the right side of the table).

2.The man came back alone (move the king back to the left) and then he took over the sack of bananas (move the king and the four to the right).

3.Next he brought back the monkey (move the king and the six to the left).

4.Then he took the lion (move the king and the ace to the right) and he returned alone (move the king to the left).

5. "Finally he took the monkey back across the river (move the king and the six)." You have solved the puzzle.

THIS
WAY
TO THE
BANANAS
?

THE STEPS AND THE MOVES

	RIVER BANK	IN BOAT	OTHER SIDE
1	man, lion, monkey, bananas		
2	lion, bananas	man, monkey to right	
3	lion, bananas	man to left	monkey
4	lion, bananas, man		
5	lion	man, bananas to right	monkey
6	lion		man, monkey, bananas
7	lion	man, monkey to left	bananas
8	lion, man, monkey		bananas
9	monkey	man, lion to right	bananas
10	monkey		man, lion, bananas
11	monkey	man to left	lion, bananas
12	no one	man, monkey to right	lion, bananas
13	no one		man, lion, monkey, bananas

HOW THIS WORKS

You are thinking clearly and **logically.** Many people will think that once something has been moved across it should stay there and they won't think of moving the monkey back and forth. *But you did!*

ALL MINE!

BOO

ALIENS AND ROBOTS

THE MAGICIAN HAS STOPPED A ROBBERY. HOW WAS IT DONE?

Your audience will watch as you tell a story and demonstrate. They see every move you make but somehow just when they think they see the aliens steal the robots, the magician shows that the robots are safe. How could it have happened? *Perplexing!*

YOU'LL NEED

1. A **paper napkin** to tear into seven balls

YOU TELL THE STORY AS YOU PERFORM

ALL
THERE!

1. This is a story about two aliens and the valuable robots they tried to steal. I'm tearing up the napkin to show you what happened. (You tear the napkin into seven pieces and squeeze each piece into a large pill sized ball. Place the balls in a row on the table.)

2. These little balls stand for the main characters in the story. Two are aliens. Five are valuable robots that the aliens would like to carry back to their own planet. I will move the aliens over to this side (Pick up two of the balls and place them on your left).

ALIENS

grr

ditto

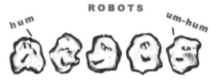

ROBOTS

hum

um-hum

3. My hands are the safe rooms where the robots are kept at night. (Show your hands.)

4. I am the guard who protects the robots at night. Somehow the aliens disguised themselves and each of them hid in a safe room. (Take one alien paper ball and put in each of your hands. The remaining five balls should be in a row on the table in front of you.)

SAFE!

HO,
HO!

5. This evening, when I came on duty, I checked each robot and put it in a safe room. (Pick up the remaining paper balls one at a time, using both hands and starting with your right hand.)

6 I knew the aliens were nearby, so before I locked the safe rooms for the night, I took the robots out of the rooms and checked to be sure they were secure. (Drop the five robots back on the table, putting them in a row).

ALL THERE

7 They were all there, so I picked them up again and returned them to the safe rooms. (Pick up the robot balls again.)

8 I didn't know that an alien was inside each room with the robots. They were about to attempt to steal the robots. But, I'm not just a guard, I'm also a magician with magic powers!"

WE'RE SAFE!

HOW'D HE DO THAT?

9 The next morning when I opened the safe rooms, I per-formed a magic spell. (Hold each fist up and blow lightly on it.) Guess what I found! All the robots were in one room while the two aliens were locked up in the other. (Open your hands and show your audience. The two aliens will be in one hand the five robots in the other.)

THIS IS WHAT YOU *REALLY* DO AS YOU TELL THE STORY

At the beginning of the story you pick up two balls for the aliens, one in each hand. Then, when you pick up the robots, you pick them up alternately, **starting with your right hand.** The audience won't realize that you actually will end up with four balls in your right hand and three in your left.

When you take the robots from the rooms to be sure they are okay, you place the balls in a row on the table, alternately from each hand, **starting with the left**, then the right until you have five balls on the table. The five are now in a row on the table but because you started with your left hand, you still have two in your right hand.

When you pick them up again, you **start with your right hand,** then your left. You have completed your "magic." When you finish the story, you should have the aliens safely captured in your left hand and the robots in your right.

HOW THE TRICK WORKS

I *TOLD* YOU SOMETHING FUNNY WAS GOING ON

This story succeeds because paper balls that look alike represent **both** the aliens and the robots. You are using basic math and simple misdirection. The magician looks up, the audience looks up and they miss what's happening down below. In this case, you used repetition and blowing on your hands to misdirect. Practice until it works smoothly.

MOBIUS BANDS

YOU CUT LOOPS OF PAPER IN HALF BUT GET SURPRISING RESULTS

You announce that you are going to perform a trick with a loop of paper. You explain that you will cut a fat loop in half and get two loops linked together. You cut the loop and hold up two loops. Now you look puzzled, but try again. You cut one of the loops in half again but this time you get one really long loop. You then cut the second loop and this time you get two loops linked together. *Amazing and amusing!*

YOU'LL NEED

1. A **strip of paper four inches wide and about two feet long** (newspaper works very well)
2. **Glue**
3. **Scissors**

HOW IT WORKS

4-INCH CUT DOWN CENTER

TWO-FOOT LONG STRIP

2-INCH CUT DOWN CENTER

BEFOREHAND

1. **Before your audience arrives,** cut the newspaper into a four inch by two-foot-long strip.

2. At one end of the strip, make a cut about four inches long down the middle. At the other end make a cut about two inches long.

3. Glue the two ends together, but before you connect them give one of the four-inch slits a half twist as shown. Then glue it. Take the other four-inch slit (right) and give it a full twist as shown. Glue it. Then let the glue dry.

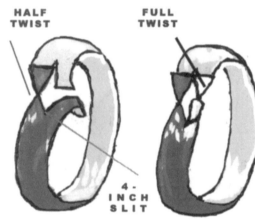

HALF TWIST

FULL TWIST

4-INCH SLIT

ONSTAGE

LOOKY!

4. **Now you are ready for your audience.** Show them your loop and explain that you are going to cut the fat loop in half and get two loops linked together

5. Cut or tear the loop the long way and hold up the two loops to show your audience. Oops. Not linked together. Scratch your head and **say**, *"I forgot to use the magic word. Let's see I think it was CA-DAB-RAH-ABRA."*

WHOOPSIE

EH?

6. Now cut the loop with the half twist down the center the long way and you'll get one long loop. Hold it up for everyone to see and **say**, *"That wasn't the right word for two loops together, was it? What do you think I did wrong?"*

7. You are likely to get suggestions from your audience. If they don't tell you, ask them. After scratching your head and looking puzzled, **say,** *"Do you think the magic word might be ABRA-CA-DAB-RAH."*

**ZINGO!
TWO
LOOPS
TOGETHER**

8. Now tear or cut the second loop in half lengthwise. This time you'll get two loops linked together. *Hoorah!* You did it!

9. Part of the fun of this trick is getting the audience involved and letting them think you are puzzled when you're actually performing the trick. Be sure to give your audience enough time to see what's happening. Hold the loops up so they can see what they look like. Sure enough, you tore a loop into two. Then when you tore one loop again, it didn't get in two, but got to be a bigger loop. And finally, when you tore the second loop in half, it got to be two loops looped together. *Neat-O.*

WHY IT WORKS

HOW
TRUE

You have just demonstrated a **mathematical concept** called a Moebius band. By cutting your loop, giving it a half-twist and reconnecting it, you have made a band that has only one side and one edge. When you're practicing this trick, run your finger around the edge of the loop with the half-twist. First it'll be on the outside and then on the inside. *Strange but true.*

FIT THROUGH THAT CARD?

NO WAY!

AMAZING EXPANDING CARD

YOU SURPRISE YOUR AUDIENCE WHEN YOU FIT *YOUR ENTIRE BODY* THROUGH A POST CARD

You **tell your audience** that you are able to fit your entire body through a hole cut in a postcard. Ask someone from the audience to try it first. Give them a scissors and an uncut card. When they give up, you show them a card that is the same size that you've already cut, then open it up and pull it over your head! *Inconceivable!*

YOU'LL NEED

1. **3 cards,** each 4 x 6 inches (postcards or file cards will do)
2. **Scissors**

FOLD CARD IN HALF
(long way)

10 CUTS ON FOLD

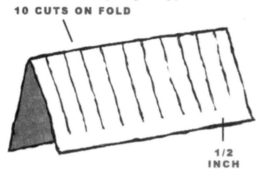

1/2 INCH

BEFORE

1. **Before your performance,** fold one of the cards in half the long way, and make ten cuts down from the fold. Leave 1/2 inch uncut at each end of each cut. Leave about 1/2 inch between each of the cuts. You might want to draw a light pencil line to guide your scissors.

CUT CENTER (EXCEPT ENDS)

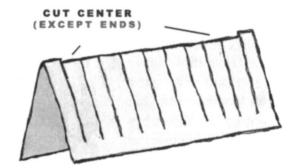

2. Cut through the center of each fold except the ones at the end.

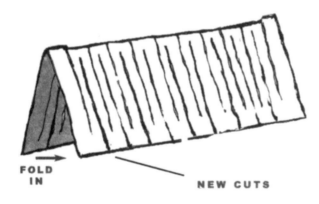

FOLD IN

NEW CUTS

3. Now, from the bottom edge of the card, make cuts between each of the cuts you have already made. Again leave about 1/2 inch uncut and don't cut the ends.

4. Now open up the paper carefully and see how much room you have. *Wow.* Carefully refold your card so you can illustrate that it was originally the same size as the uncut card. You are ready for your trick.

ONSTAGE

5. **When your audience is watching** and you are ready to perform, call for a volunteer. If you don't get a volunteer, pick someone in the audience and give him or her a scissors and the uncut card. Let him or her try for a while. If he or she seems to want to keep trying, let your volunteer sit in the audience and work on the problem while you do another trick.

6. Now call your volunteer back up and ask if he or she has solved the problem. When he or she tells you he or she is puzzled, show your card. Hold the volunteer's card or an uncut one together with your card so the audience and your volunteer can see that they are the same size. Then unfold your card and pull it over your body. *Wow!*

WIZARDLY   LOOK AT THAT!

WHY THIS WORKS

Most of us believe that a flat, paper card cannot be stretched beyond its finished size. In this case, with your scissors, you have changed the mathematical variable of **size.** You have greatly expanded the dimensions of the card by making carefully planned cuts. It's an interesting lesson in mathematics but don't try to explain it to your audience and don't repeat it. Remember you're the *magician.*

F - F - FAST!

Z O O P !

RACING CAR

A PICTURE OF A CAR THAT MOVES SO FAST NO ONE CAN CATCH IT!

You ask someone from the audience to draw a picture of a fast car. Then you perform a magic spell that makes the picture **so fast** that when it is dropped no one can *catch it!*

YOU WILL NEED

1. A **sheet of paper** (half of an 8 fi x 11)
2. A **crayon**
3. A **table.**

DRAW, DRAW

HOW IT WORKS

1. Ask a volunteer from the audience to draw a fast car. Give your volunteer paper and crayon. When he/she has drawn the picture, ask the artist to tell you about the car. What kind is it? How fast can it go? Would you be able to catch it with an ordinary car?

2. Then tell the audience that you are going to give the pictured car magical powers to be really fast. Close your eyes and hold the paper to your forehead while mumbling to yourself. Turn around twice and then ask the artist to see if he/she can catch the car.

3. Have your artist lay his/her arm on the table with an open hand over the edge. Tell your volunteer that you will drop the picture and he/she will try to catch it before it drops to the floor.

HAND OPEN, THUMB AND FINGERS SLIGHTLY SPREAD

EASY!

4.Offer a prize if the artist can catch the paper before it falls to the floor. The prize might be a candy bar or a dollar bill.

5. Hold the paper inside of the artist's open hand with about half a sheet or less above the hand. Your artist should not be able to tell when you're going to drop the paper. Be sure the volunteer's hand is not touching the paper but is loosely open around it. Drop the racing car drawing. *Surprise!* He/she won't be able to catch it.

INSERT PAPER INSIDE HAND. HAND SHOULD BE OPEN

ZOOP!

6. Someone else from the audience is likely to think they could catch the paper, so let that person try. *Astounding.* Now, move on to your next trick. No more demonstrations.

WHY IT WORKS

NOT SO EASY

Gravity makes objects fall faster and faster. The person trying to catch the paper won't know when it will drop, and first has to see it moving. Then the person's brain must register the action and signal the fingers that they need to catch the paper. It is almost impossible for someone to be able to process the information that quickly and react fast enough to beat the gravitational pull.

YO!

CAPTURED STRENGTH

YOU TAKE AWAY THE STRENGTH OF A LARGER AND STRONGER PERSON

Although you may not be the strongest person in the room, **you are able to take strength** from others. One of the biggest and strongest appearing people in your audience is not able to lift you as long as you say a magic word and touch a special nerve under his chin.

YOU'LL NEED

1. A **volunteer**
2. One of your **fingers**

1. **You tell the audience** that you are magically able to take away the strength of someone who is stronger than you are. Pick someone who is obviously strong and ask him if he thinks he can lift you. If he says yes, invite him to come on your stage.

2. Tell your audience that you will find a special nerve under the chin that takes away strength. Now you will touch the volunteer under the chin. Spend a little time touching areas under the volunteer's chin with your forefinger, as if you needed to find a special spot. Don't be shy.

3. Invite the volunteer to grasp your arms or under your arms (choose a spot that isn't ticklish). Tell him you'll let him know when you want him to lift you up.

CADABRA

4. With your finger under his chin, gently push his chin up as you **say** "*Cadabra, now lift*" Be careful: you don't want to use a lot of pressure. Push just enough to move his head up, just before you say your magic words.

5. He won't be able to lift you from the floor and you will have demonstrated your magical ability to steal strength from stronger people.

WHY THIS WORKS

EASY!

There is no magic nerve under the chin that allows you to make another person weak. But you must spend time looking for the right spot and saying a magic word to draw attention away from what is actually happening. In order to lift you, the volunteer must lean forward. He can't do this when you are pushing his chin up. When his head is pushed up and back by your finger, he is **off balance** and not able to exert his normal strength. Be quick: If you spend too much time, he may discover your secret before you ask him to do the trick.

GAINING WEIGHT

YOU SHOW THAT YOU CAN MAGICALLY MAKE YOURSELF *LIGHT* OR *HEAVY*

You ask two strong people to lift you as you stand with your arms bent, hands on your shoulders and arms at your sides. They lift you easily. Then after you appear to say a magic spell, you again bend your arms and put your hands on your shoulders. This time they aren't able to lift you. *Startling!*

YOU'LL NEED

1. Yourself
2. Two strong volunteers

SCOPE THIS OUT!

1. You begin by telling your audience that as a magician, you are able to use magic to make your body lighter or heavier.

2 Ask for two volunteers from the audience. Explain that you'll you'll need two strong people to lift you.

LIGHTER

3. When your volunteers step up, put your hands on your shoulders, arms bent and elbows at your side. Your arms should be tight against your body. Put a volunteer on each side of you, have them hold you by the elbows and lift together. If you have really strong people, they should be able to lift you *easily*.

ARMS TIGHT AGAINST BODY

HANDS ON SHOULDERS

4. Then you explain that you can make yourself heavier using magic. You back away from your volunteers, turn around twice. Then facing the audience, bend your arms and **say** *"Heavy, heavy grows my body"* as you blow on the inside curve of your arms, opposite your elbows.

HEAVIER

HANDS
CLOSE TO NECK

ELBOWS
OUT
IN FRONT

5. Put your hands back on your shoulders, but slide them up closer to your neck (you can even clasp your hands in back of your neck.) Move your elbows out in front of you, up and away from your sides. Now ask your volunteers to each hold an elbow and lift. This time they won't be able to lift you.

6. Practice this until you're able to do the movements quickly and easily, without repositioning your arms and hands several times.

WHY THIS WORKS

ELBOWS
OUT DETAIL

OUT

The second time your volunteers try to lift you, you've changed the angle of your elbows and the **center of gravity** of your body. When your elbows are at your side, next to your body, your center of gravity is centered in your body and it makes you easy to lift. When you move your elbows in front of your body, the applied lift force is away from your center of gravity. The more the distance is increased away from your body, the more force you'll need to overcome the resistance of your weight.

BROOMS FLY

(DON'T THEY?)

EVERYONE KNOWS THAT MAGICAL BROOMS SHOULD FLY. WHY WON'T THESE *MOVE?*

You explain that although some witches and other magicians can make brooms fly, you can magically stop them. You ask two volunteers to each hold a broom. Then you make a few turns of a rope around the broom handles and easily hold on to the end of the rope while the strong volunteers are unable to pull the brooms apart.

YOU'LL NEED

1. **2 brooms**
2. **A rope** about 4 or 5 feet long

1. **Before your performance**, practice assembling the brooms and the rope. Use a tight knot that won't pull apart. Be sure to untie the rope before you perform.

FLYING BROOM ?

2. **When your audience is gathered**, ask for two volunteers who are strong enough to move a broom around the floor. After they come forward and have been introduced, bring out your two brooms. Give a broom to each one. Ask how many in the audience have heard of brooms that fly. (Do this after you have volunteers because they may not volunteer if they think you're going to make them fly with the brooms.)

3. Then explain that these are just two ordinary brooms that sweep. Ask the volunteers to demonstrate how they work sweeping.

4. Now pick the rope off your table. Explain that it is the rope that performs magic, not the brooms. Have the volunteers stand beside you with the brooms. Ask them to move the brooms toward each other and away. Have them stand a few feet apart and hold the brooms toward each other about 6 to 9 inches apart.

ROPE

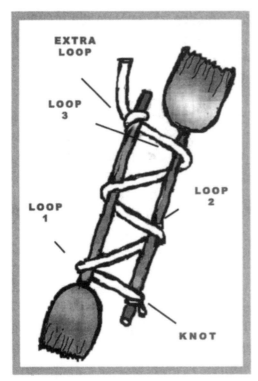

5. Tell the audience that you will hypnotize the brooms with the magic rope. Tie one end of the rope to the bottom of a broom handle. Lace the rope around the broom handles (see the illustration). Three loops around both handles should be just about right. Add an extra loop to the top of the handle nearest you for security.

6. Hold on to the end of the rope with one hand and **say** in a singsong voice *"Magic rope won't you put these brooms to sleep."* At the same time wave your free hand over the brooms.

7. Ask the volunteers to pull the brooms straight apart (no twist-ing). Hold tight to the rope and the two volunteers will be unable to pull the brooms. Explain that you have used the magic rope to make the brooms sleep. Ask each volunteer to **say** *"Wake up broom!"* while you let go of the rope. Remove the rope and ask each volunteer to lay the broom on the floor.

WHY THIS WORKS

With the rope you have created a form of **double pulley.** This is used every day for lifting and lowering heavy boxes, cranes and machinery. For your magic show, each time you wrap the rope around the broom handles, you increase the distance the rope has to be pulled. When you pull on the rope you apply a small force over a long distance. This multiplies power. That's why a single magician *without force* can keep the broom handles from moving.

INVISIBLE GUARD

FILL A GLASS WITH WATER, TURN IT UPSIDE DOWN BUT *NO WATER* RUNS OUT

You tell the audience that you can turn a glass filled with water upside down and the water will stay inside the glass. You fill the glass with water, put a piece of newspaper on top of the glass, command *"Water Stay!"* and turn the glass upside down. The water does not **run out.** *Beyond belief!*

YOU WILL NEED

1. A sink with running water (or a large pan and a pitcher of water)

2. A small glass, like a juice glass

3. Pieces of newspaper that are an inch or more larger than the glass on each side. (You can also use a sturdy paper towel, construction paper or a plain piece of paper)

1. This is a trick that is best done outside on a warm day or someplace where splashed water will not hurt the audience, the room or the furniture.

2. Hold up the glass and the paper. Turn on the faucet. Explain that through magic you will make water stay in the glass without running out. If running water is not convenient, use a large pitcher filled with water and a large pan to catch spills.

3. Invite a member of the audience to try to do it. If no one volunteers, it would be good to have a friend agree to come forward and try. Keep one sheet of paper dry and away from the rest so you'll have something left to use when it's your turn.

4. After several attempts to make the water stay in the glass, without success, you (the magician) step forward and show how it is done.

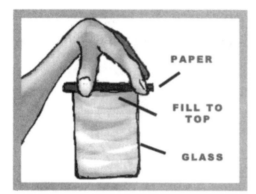

5. Fill the glass all the way to the top. Set the glass on a flat surface and put the paper on top of it. If the glass is filled, the paper will get wet. This only helps to seal the top, so don't worry.

6. **Command** *"Water Stay!"* in a loud voice, carefully turning the glass upside down while holding the paper on top of the glass. Carefully remove your hand and the water will stay in the glass, sealed by the newspaper.

WHY IT WORKS

This succeeds because of **air pressure.** The air pressure pushing up against the paper is stronger than the water pressure pushing down. The glass needs to be full so no air will be inside. The water stays in the glass. When the paper gets wet it only seals the glass tighter and makes sure no air pressure gets inside the glass to force the water out.

GLASSES OF WATER

A PUZZLE EASY TO SOLVE. OR IS IT?

You use **six glasses** to present a difficult problem. When you solve it, everyone will think they too could have solved it. Then you present a harder problem.

YOU'LL NEED

1. Six glasses
2. A pitcher of water

1. Set six glasses in a row on a table in front of your audience. Tell them that you have a puzzle for them to solve. Pour water into the first three glasses and leave the last three empty.

1   2   3   4   5   6

2. Now ask them to see if they can arrange the glasses so they will be *full, empty, full, empty, full, empty*. They can only touch **one** glass to do this.

3. Someone in the audience may know how to do this or think of the answer. If they do praise them, ask if anyone else thought of the answer and give him or her praise too.

4. If no one thinks of the answer, you demonstrate. You pick up the second glass, pour the water into the fifth glass and then return glass two, now *empty,* to its original place. The glasses are now in proper sequence. Wow!

THAT'S IT?

1   2   3   4   5   6

HOW THE TRICK WORKS

You can see this puzzle has a **logical answer** and you'll wonder why you didn't think of it immediately. The reason that it might take a while to come up with the answer is that when you talk about arranging the glasses everyone starts thinking about moving the glasses instead of just the water. Of course, if someone rearranges the glasses, they have to touch more than one glass.

THREE
THIS
TIME?

PUZZLING GLASSES

A MORE DIFFICULT GLASS PUZZLE. YOU CAN DO IT, BUT ALAS, NO ONE ELSE CAN. *EVEN WHEN YOU SHOW THEM*

You show the audience an arrangement of only three glasses. Then you quickly demonstrate how to arrange the glasses right side up in three moves. You invite a volunteer or volunteers to try. After each attempt, you patiently show them how it's done, but no one else can solve the puzzle. *Amazing.*

YOU'LL NEED

1. Three glasses (water or juice size will do nicely.) These must all be the same.

2. A table or shelf on which to perform your amazing trick.

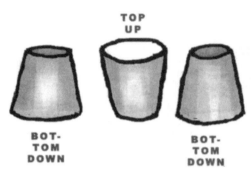

TOP
UP

BOT-
TOM
DOWN

BOT-
TOM
DOWN

1. You arrange three glasses in a row in front of the audience. It works well if you can stand in back of a table and the audience is in front of it. You arrange the glasses so each end glass is bottom up and the center glass is top up.

2. You tell your audience that the challenge is to turn over two glasses at a time, make three moves, and end with all glasses top up. Then you quickly make the following moves:

3. **First move:** Turn your hands so the thumbs are down and turn over the two glasses on the right. You'll now have an arrangement of bottom, bottom, top up. *(below)*

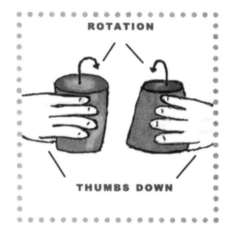

ROTATION

THUMBS DOWN

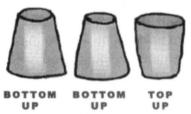

BOTTOM
UP

BOTTOM
UP

TOP
UP

NEVER
HAPPEN

TOP UP   BOTTOM BOTTOM

4. **Second move:** With your thumbs down, turn over the two glasses at each end of the row. Now you should have top up, bottom, bottom. You have one move to go. Can you make it?

5. **Third move:** With your thumbs down, turn over the two bottom up glasses. Now you now have all of the glasses top side, or right side, up. *Amazing!* And so *easy.*

ZOW! SUCCESS!

TOP UP   TOP UP   TOP UP

MY TURN?
ULP!

TOP UP   BOTTOM UP   TOP UP

6. Now turn over the middle glass and invite one or two people from the audience to try. Emphasize that it should be done in exactly three moves. Whoever tries, will not be able to do the trick so you rearrange it, do it once more and invite another volunteer to try. Now go on to the next trick.

WHY THIS WORKS

BEATS ME!

You are **misleading** your audience. When you start the trick, the two end glasses are bottom up. When you arrange them for your volunteer, the two end glasses will be right side up and the middle will be bottom up.

If the volunteer is able to copy your exact moves, she or he will end up with all of the glasses bottom up instead of upright. Then you just turn the middle glass over and you again have the workable puzzle with the two end glasses bottom up. Don't repeat this more than one or two times.

LEAKING BOTTLE

WATER SQUIRTS OUT OF A BOTTLE WITH A HOLE IN IT, UNTIL THE MAGICIAN MAKES IT STOP

You puncture a plastic bottle with a needle. You tell your audience that even with a hole in the bottle it is possible to fill it above the hole and not lose water. A volunteer fills the bottle with water, but it always leaks. Finally, you demonstrate how it's done. You fill the bottle while holding a finger over the hole and say, "Water, stay!" in a commanding voice. You remove your finger but the bottle doesn't leak. *Astounding.*

YOU'LL NEED

1. A **plastic bottle** (like a soft drink bottle) with a cover
2. A **needle**
3. **Water**
4. A **strong helper**

This is a trick that is best done outside on a warm day or someplace where splashed water will not hurt the audience, the room or the furniture. Have fun!

WILL IT HOLD WATER?

1. Show the empty bottle to the audience. **Ask:** *If I make a hole in this bottle, will it hold water? Or will it all run out?* Tell them: *"It really is possible — with magic."*

2. Use the needle or ask your helper to use the needle and make a hole near the bottom of the bottle.

POKE!
POKE!

3.Ask someone from your audience if they can make the bottle hold water without leaking and without stopping the hole. Give them the bottle and water to fill it. Usually someone will think they know how to do it. (If indoors, be sure the bottle is over a sink or a pan when it is filled because the water is going to run out the hole.)

EW!

WATER STAY

4. Finally, the magician will take the bottle. You hold your finger over the hole while you fill the bottle all the way to the top. Put on the cover and **command**, *"Water Stay!"* You take your finger from the hole and the bottle will hold water. *Amazing!*

When you do the trick, *be sure you* **fill the bottle all the way to the top** *and put the cover on tightly before you remove your finger from the hole.*

WHY IT WORKS

THAT'S IT?

Air pressure is strong. When the bottle is only partly full or uncapped, air pressure will force the water out of the hole. But when you fill and cap the bottle, there is no air pressure to push down on the water. That's why water *doesn't* run out.

THE
MAGIC
KNOT

CAN YOU
TIE
A KNOT
WITHOUT
LETTING GO?

You challenge your audience to tie a knot while holding both ends of a rope or scarf and without letting go. Let your friends participate and try this. Then, after two or three tries, you step forward and do it! What a surprise!

YOU WILL NEED

1. A **scarf**, shoestring, or lightweight rope.about three feet long.

LOOKIE HERE!

1. Lay the rope or rolled up scarf out lengthwise so that it is easy to pick up. Let others try to make a knot without letting go of either end.

NOTHING IN EITHER HAND

2. Cross your arms. Wiggle your fingers. *Smile*.

TRICKY?

3. Without uncrossing your arms, pick up an end in each hand. You'll use your right hand to pick up the left end of the string. Your left hand will pick up the right end of the string.

4. **Uncross** your arms. A knot will appear in the rope. You have tied a knot without moving your hands from either end.

Practice this until you can do it easily and smoothly. Once you've done this trick, the people in your audience will start to learn how it is done so only do it one time. Don't let them talk you into doing it again. Perhaps now is a good time to go to your next trick, the Dancing Hanky.

WHY IT WORKS

FUN, HUH?

This illusion is simply a matter of allowing your mind to think in a way that's slightly different than everyone else. Many great inventors and artists use ideas that are simple but unusual.

WHERE'S THE KNOT?

POOF

VANISHING KNOT

A KNOT TIED IN A SCARF DISAPPEARS WHEN YOU BLOW ON IT

You show the audience a scarf and tie a knot in it. Then, before their eyes, you blow on the scarf and the knot disappears. *Unbelievable!*

YOU'LL NEED

1. A lightweight silk scarf
2. A practice shoestring

1. You can practice this with a shoestring until you learn it. The illustrations show a shoestring because it's easier to follow the steps. Shoestrings tie well, but scarves make the tied knot appear more genuine. If you have several scarves, try various sizes and weights until you find the one that seems to work best for you.

2. With a scarf, grasp the diagonal corners of the scarf and twirl the scarf until it looks like a loose rope.

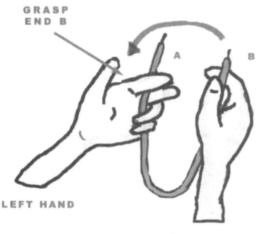

GRASP
END B

LEFT HAND

RIGHT HAND

3. We'll call the ends A and B. Grasp End **A** in your left hand between your index and middle fingers, your ring and little fingers curled around the scarf. With your right hand, bring End **B** over End A and grasp it between your thumb and the side of the index finger of your left hand. This forms a large loop.

4. Put your right hand through the loop. Grasp End **A** with your right hand. Bring the middle finger of your left hand forward over End **B** section of the loop.

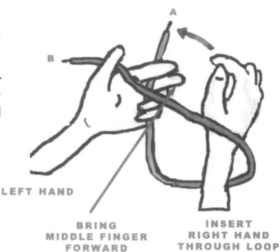

LEFT HAND

BRING
MIDDLE FINGER
FORWARD

INSERT
RIGHT HAND
THROUGH LOOP

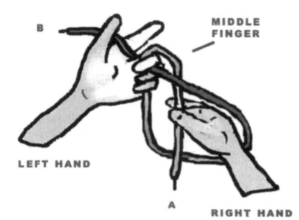

5. With your right hand, bring End **A** over the left middle finger and inside the loop.

6. With your left middle finger, do a secret twist and pull a small loop from End **B** through the little loop you're holding. (This might look like a chain or a loop for knitting).

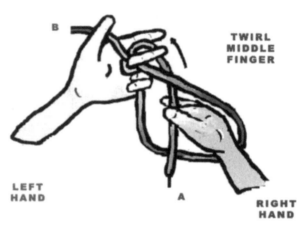

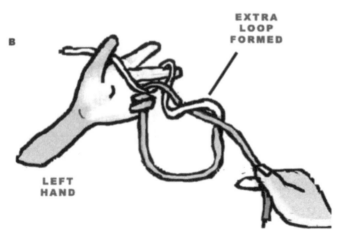

7. Now you actually have created a slipknot. You secretly keep your middle or ring finger in that small loop until you slide it into a knot that will hold its shape. This won't show if you are careful to **show only the backs of your hands to the audience.**

8. Now slip your finger out and the knot will continue to hold. You should be able to hold the knotted scarf before the audience, only holding on each end of the scarf.

9. Now blow on the knot as you pull on each end of the scarf. You can even give the scarf an extra **flick** as you demonstrate to your audience that the knot has vanished. *Amazing.*

WHY THIS WORKS

You are deceiving the audience by hiding the fact that you have secretly tied a **slipknot.** The scarf holds the shape of the knot better so it is less hard to see that it is not a true knot. It also allows you to slip your finger out and show the knot to your audience before you perform your "magic."

THE MYSTERIOUS DANCING HANKY

YOU MAKE A HANKY STAND UP AND MOVE ON YOUR COMMAND

You **take an *ordinary* cloth handkerchief** and put it under your spell. Upon your command, it will move right, left and around. It even will sit up straight and follow your finger. *Unbelievable!*

YOU WILL NEED

1. A **small cloth handkerchief** or **napkin**

1.Take out a small cloth napkin or hand-kerchief and *shake it* to show it is just a plain piece of cloth.

SHAKE SHAKE

2. Hold the upper left corner between your left thumb and forefin-ger. With your right hand, grasp the right hem about halfway down *between* the two corners.

MID-

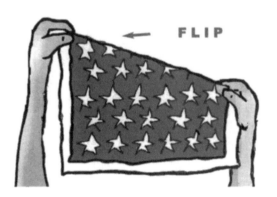

← FLIP

3. Let the hanky flip over. Hold the cloth in front of you. Twirl the cloth between your hands until it is rolled tightly, almost like a rope.

4. Hold the hanky with your left hand. Move your right hand above your left so it is directly in line. Without allowing any of the twists to unroll, move your right hand up until it holds the rope-like cloth in the middle. Pull up on the hanky just a little with your right hand and then let go. The cloth will stand straight up like it was a stick

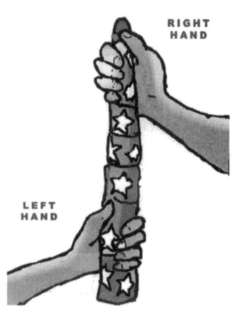

RIGHT HAND

LEFT HAND

5. Move your left thumb up and down. See how the hanky moves from left to right as you move your thumb.

MOVE THUMB UP TO TILT HANKY TO ONE SIDE

WOW!

LEFT

MOVE THUMB DOWN TO TILT HANKY TO THE OTHER SIDE

RIGHT

Practice your thumb movements so that you don't move anything but the left thumb (no wrist or arm movements) and so that it's not noticeable by your audience.

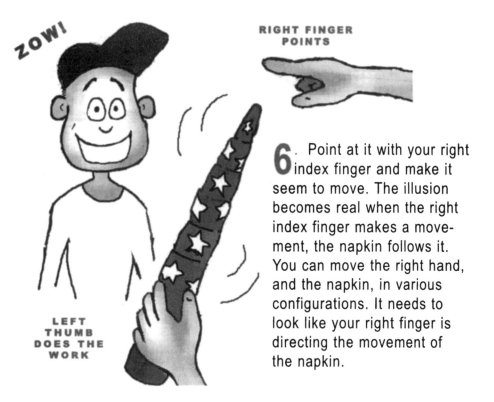

ZOW!

LEFT
THUMB
DOES THE
WORK

RIGHT FINGER
POINTS

6. Point at it with your right index finger and make it seem to move. The illusion becomes real when the right index finger makes a movement, the napkin follows it. You can move the right hand, and the napkin, in various configurations. It needs to look like your right finger is directing the movement of the napkin.

7. After a short demonstration, crush the napkin by bringing your hand down on the top of the cloth. Then quickly bring your right hand up, using your right fingers and thumb to straighten the cloth. If you practice this movement well, the napkin will seem to straighten all by itself.

SQUISH!

HOW'D SHE DO THAT?

ZOWIE!

8. Finally, shake out the cloth to show the audience that it's only a napkin without anything to make it more solid. Wave it around to show that there's nothing up your sleeve, or, up in the cloth. *Applause!*

BEATS ME!

WHY THIS WORKS

When you twist the cloth it changes **form.** It becomes thicker, heavier and more solid. It then holds its shape and no longer drapes like a thin piece of cloth. Apply pressure secretly and it moves. The tricky part is when you use your right finger and the cloth seems to follow it along on your command. *Like magic!*

OH, OH

MYSTERIOUS
VASE
OF
INDIA

**AN ORDINARY
ROPE
MAGICALLY
STAYS IN A
VASE
WITHOUT
ANYTHING
TO HOLD IT**

The magician inserts a rope in a small vase. Then a strange force takes over and locks the rope inside the vase with no apparent reason. By merely holding onto the rope, you can turn the vase upside down, lift it and swing it back and forth. Finally, when you cause the "spell" to be broken, the rope and vase return to normal. The rope can be removed from the vase and when inspected, both appear to be ordinary objects.

YOU'LL NEED

1. A bud **vase** (or a salad dressing bottle that you have painted to make it opaque. Put magic symbols or your own special design on it.) A clear vase won't work.

2. A **rope**, about 2 feet long, and about half the size of the neck of the vase (it is best if it's thicker and stiffer than the ropes you use to tie knots.)

3. A **small rubber or cork ball** a little larger than *half the neck* of the vase, so it'll easily roll in and out of the vase.

1. Start with your secret ball inside the vase. Show the rope and the vase to the audience. (You will know from your practice how far you can tip the vase without letting the ball roll out.) Now put the rope inside the vase and pull it out to show the audience that it slides easily and you can't wedge it in the vase and make it stay. Finally, at the end of your demonstration, slide the rope into the vase until its end rests near the bottom of the vase.

ROPE SLIDES IN AND OUT

TURN ROPE & VASE UPSIDE DOWN

2. Slowly turn the rope and the vase upside down. Hold the vase in one hand and the end of the rope in the other. Now the secret ball should roll between the neck of the vase and the rope.

X-RAY VIEW

BALL SLIDES DOWN TO LOCK ROPE

3. To be sure that the rope will stay in place, give it a small tug before you let go. This will lodge the ball firmly in place. Gradually release the rope as you lift the upside down vase. To the audience, the rope will seem to be held in place, magically.

4. Now you can hold on to the free end of the rope and release the grip on the vase. You will be able to swing the vase back and forth while you only hold on to the rope.

SWING SWING

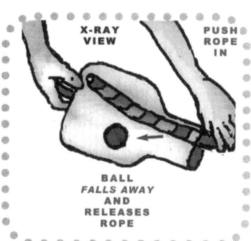

X-RAY VIEW

PUSH ROPE IN

BALL FALLS AWAY AND RELEASES ROPE

5. Finally, when you have impressed your audience with the "magic force" that keeps the rope in the bottle, you can release the rope by holding the vase in one hand, the rope in the other, and pushing in slightly on the rope. This will release the ball and allow it to fall to the bottom of the vase.

6. Then you will be able to pull the rope from the vase. Hand the rope to someone in the audience. Turn up the vase and, showing the back of your hands to the audience, secretly allow the ball to roll into your palm. Of course the audience will see only the vase and the back of your hand.

7. Now you can pass the rope and the vase around to be inspected by the audience. Some will try to do the trick, but of course, only you know the magic secret.

WHY THIS WORKS

You have completed your magic trick using a device frequently employed by magicians. You **palmed** the secret ball, slipping it into the palm of your hand, so the audience did not see it. They didn't know you had that secret ball inside the vase to make your magic trick work.

Hint: Try various balls until you find one that works just right in your vase. Little toy balls or small balls for kittens may work. If you can't find the right one, try having one carved out of cork.

THE MAGIC CABINET

YOU MAKE PEOPLE APPEAR AND DISAPPEAR!

You and an assistant **push a large cabinet** into the room. You demonstrate that it is empty. Then you make another assistant disappear from the box and then reappear again. *Incredible!*

YOU'LL NEED

1. A **large empty cardboard box** (the box has to be big enough to hold a quick moving person of about your own age). One that held a new refrigerator, stove or large TV set will work fine.

2. An **adult helper** with something sharp to cut openings in the box.

3. Tape, paper, paste, crayons and magic markers to decorate the box. Stars, moons are magic symbols.

BEFORE THE EVENT

With the help of your adult helper, tape shut any wrong openings and cut new openings in the front and back of your box. Decorate the box with paper and paste, crayons and magic markers.

HOW IT WORKS

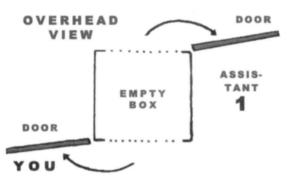

OVERHEAD VIEW

DOOR

EMPTY BOX

ASSISTANT 1

DOOR

YOU

IT'S EMPTY

1. You and your assistant open the front door and then the back door to show that the cabinet is empty. Close both doors.

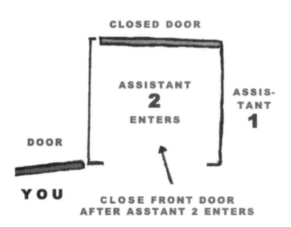

CLOSED DOOR

ASSISTANT 2 ENTERS

ASSISTANT 1

DOOR

YOU

CLOSE FRONT DOOR AFTER ASSTANT 2 ENTERS

2. Bring your second assistant forward. Open the front door only. Assistant Two steps into the cabinet, the magician closes the front door, waves his arms, **says** SHAZAM. Say something like *"I hope this works. I've only done this a few times."*

3. Assistant One opens the back door *just seconds* before you open the front door. Assistant Two slips out and stands **behind** the open back door so the inside of the box is empty. Because the back door goes all the way to the floor, the audience won't see Assistant Two. Practice so Assistant One seems to open the back door at the same time you open the front *door.*

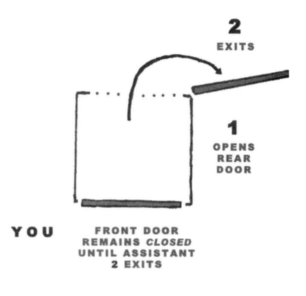

2
EXITS

1
OPENS
REAR
DOOR

YOU

FRONT DOOR
REMAINS *CLOSED*
UNTIL ASSISTANT
2 EXITS

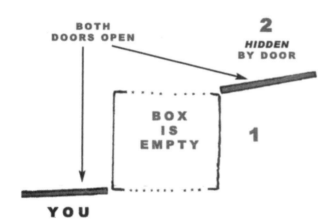

BOTH
DOORS OPEN

2
*HIDDEN
BY DOOR*

BOX
IS
EMPTY

1

YOU

4. The magician reveals an **empty box.** Assistant Two has disappeared. *Wow! (Actually, the door hides assistant Two from the audience's view.)*

5. For a few moments, you and Assistant One look around and talk. Assistant One might say, *"Are you going to be able to get her back?"* You could say, *"I hope so, but I haven't tried it with real people before. I just tried it with this new book."* Then you could show them a really torn and dirty book that you've had for a long time.

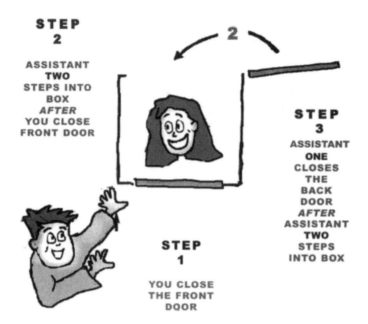

STEP 2

ASSISTANT **TWO** STEPS INTO BOX *AFTER* YOU CLOSE FRONT DOOR

STEP 3

ASSISTANT **ONE** CLOSES THE BACK DOOR *AFTER* ASSISTANT **TWO** STEPS INTO BOX

STEP 1

YOU CLOSE THE FRONT DOOR

6. When you and Assistant One close the doors, Assistant Two will step back in, just as the back door closes behind her. The magician might **say**, *"I hope I remember the magic word to get her back. Was it Mazam?"* The magician and Assistant One peek inside the cabinet without opening the door all the way for the audience and **say**, *"No, that didn't work."*

7. Finally, you **say**, *SHAZAM* , and throw open the front door. Assistant Two will reappear *inside* the cabinet!

SHE'S BACK!

YOU OPEN FRONT DOOR

8. The big finish: You and Assistant Two step forward for a well-deserved bow. *Applause!*

WHY IT WORKS

You are using **illusion** to make the audience think that the box is empty, that the doors are opening at the same time, and that there is no possible place Assistant Two could have gone. Your conversation with the audience distracts them and they won't watch as closely as if you did everything quietly. You need to practice this a lot or your audience will catch you.

LIKE PULLING A RABBIT OUT OF A HAT, ONLY NICER

INDEX

MY MAGIC NOTES

Things to remember about my performances, tricks, equipment and the people who helped me

1 . . . .

2 . . . .

3 . . . .

4 . . . .

5 . . . .

6 . . . .

7 . . . .

8 . . . .

9 . . . .

10 . . . .

11 . . . .

12 . . . .

13 . . . .

14 . . . .

15 . . . .

16 . . . .

MY MAGIC NOTES
continued

17 . . . .

18 . . . .

19 . . . .

20 . . . .

21 . . . .

22 . . . .

23 . . . .

24 . . . .

25 . . . .

26 . . . .

27 . . . .

23 . . . .

24 . . . .

25 . . . .

26 . . . .

HAVE
FUN!

27 . . . .

28 . . . .

If it's not fun, it's not really MAGIC